IMAGES
of America

FORT WASHINGTON

FORT WASHINGTON.[1]

Fort Washington, a 19th-century fort located in southern Maryland off the Potomac River, was designed to provide the greatest firepower along the Potomac River. The fort was built to guard the water approach to the Capital City and Alexandria, Virginia. The structure was completed in 1824 and is one of the few surviving seacoast fortifications. The U.S. Army has used the fort for an officer candidate school and a hospital, and it is now a park under the management of the National Park Service. (Courtesy National Archives and Records Administration.)

IMAGES
of America

FORT WASHINGTON

Nathania Branch-Miles, Jane Taylor Thomas,
and Beverly Babin Woods

Published by Arcadia Publishing
Charleston SC, Chicago IL, Portsmouth NH, San Francisco CA

Printed in Great Britain

Library of Congress Catalog Card Number: 2005930994

For all general information contact Arcadia Publishing at:
Telephone 843-853-2070
Fax 843-853-0044
E-mail sales@arcadiapublishing.com
For customer service and orders:
Toll-Free 1-888-313-2665

Visit us on the Internet at www.arcadiapublishing.com

Fort Washington is located southeast of the national's capital off Indian Head Highway (Maryland Route 210). The fort is situated on the Potomac River, directly across from Mount Vernon, Virginia, the home of George Washington, the fort's namesake. In 1809, the first fort, Fort Warburton, was built on the property of Col. William Digges to protect the entrance to the Capital City until it was ordered to be destroyed in 1814. (Courtesy National Archives and Records Administration.)

CONTENTS

ACKNOWLEDGMENTS

The authors would like to take this opportunity to acknowledge and express thanks to the many people who contributed valuable history and pictures to Images of America: *Fort Washington*. Many thanks are given to Jo Proctor, office manager of Rosecroft Raceway, who gave us the unknown history of the Rosecroft Raceway, the county's only harness raceway; and to William Herndon of the College Park Aviation Museum for his knowledge and history of the county's public and private airports, such as Potomac Airfield (formerly Rose Valley Airport, also formerly Prince George's Airpark). A special thanks goes to Carolyn C. Rowe, who was very helpful throughout the project. The authors would be remiss if they did not acknowledge the assistance given them by Ranger Barbara Waddington of the Fort Washington National Park Service, the Prince George's County Historical Society's historians, and the librarians at the Prince George's County Memorial Library, who also shared pictures and histories of various times and places. The authors also recognize the role of the Library of Congress Prints and Photographs Division Historic American Buildings Survey (HABS), which provided the historical images of buildings, homes, and remnants of a time gone by. A special thanks goes to Imara A. Miles, who gave special assistance collecting history and photographs of the Fort Washington area. We would like to also thank Marion DiLorenzo for providing materials on Tantallon. Finally, we extend gratitude to Maurice Thomas, who provided professional expertise in information management and photography, as well as Clifford Wood for taking pictures of markers, signs, and buildings of Fort Washington.

INTRODUCTION

The visual images of Fort Washington reflected in these pages tell a pictorial history of a 17th-century Colonial community that started as a collection of tracts of land. Fort Washington is located in the southern sector of Prince George's County across from Fort Hunt in Alexandria, Virginia. Fort Hunt is another historic military facility that was constructed to protect Federal City, also known as Capital City and later the city of Washington, D.C. Agriculture was the industry of the day, with rural farms and villages that transitioned into a modern-day, culturally diverse urban community of homes, businesses, and people of the 21st century.

The Fort Washington Colonial community started with a few pioneer families who moved from southern Maryland (St. Mary's County) by traveling up the Patuxent and Potomac Rivers to take advantage of landownership opportunities. The passion of the early settlers was "land accumulation" and "land-trading." Few tracts in the region failed to change hands as value increased with the rise of the population. In many cases, land was accumulated through the marriages of the prominent families of the region. Alliances were made as a means of keeping tracts of land together or adding to the family wealth.

Until 1634, the early inhabitants of southern Maryland were Native Americans, when approximately 200 colonists arrived from England with Leonard Calvert, brother of Lord Baltimore. Living conditions were considered to be primitive; however, the woods were free of underbrush, and there was plenty of deer, fish, and other wild life to hunt for food. The Europeans came to the new colony because of the opportunities to own their own land, but many others looked at it as a chance for religious freedom. In 1692, the Church of England was established. Catholics were allowed to worship in private homes by invitation but not permitted to build a church. Prince George's County was incorporated on April 23, 1695, on St. George's Day, according to Kathleen A. Kellock's *Colonial Piscataway in Maryland*. Lumber and gristmills, as well as plantations and farms, were the mainstay. Towns were established along the Patuxent and Potomac Rivers near the larger plantations at Digges Point, Warburton Manor, Frankland, Battersea, Thompson's Rest, Little Hall, Batchelor Harbour, and other nearby tracts.

The first known communities in the Fort Washington area consisted of family-owned tracts or parcels of land that included the plantations of the Diggeses, Addisons, Hattons, Darnells, Lowes, Rozers, Carrolls, and Neals. Slave labor was introduced into the economy to clear the vast forests and to work the large tobacco farms. According to the Maryland historic records in the August 1776 census, the total numbers of whites living in Prince George's County was 4,986 compared to 3,400 slaves.

The towns of Nottingham, Queen Anne, Piscataway, and Broad Creek did not grow as quickly or as large as Upper Marlboro, but they did become thriving little places in themselves: centers for buying, selling, and socializing along the Patuxent and Potomac Rivers. In 1705 and 1706, the Maryland General Assembly established five towns; only Mill Town failed to develop. As the northern sections of the county were settled, towns developed there, too.

The southern area of Prince George's County did not participate in the War of 1812. The anticipated war efforts played an important role in the development of forts in and around Prince George's County. However, no part of the war was fought in the southern sector. In August 1814, the British sailed up the Patuxent to Benedict and began a march into Prince George's County through Nottingham, Upper Marlboro, and Forestville all the way to Bladensburg, where the British Army defeated an ill-prepared army of American defenders. The British marched into Washington and burned the city.

In the 1840s, Fort Washington was remodeled to correct deficiencies in the original design. From 1875 until 1921, the fort was made a military post and was headquarters for the Defenses of the Potomac. By 1890, work started on the Endicott gun batteries. In 1906, all work was completed on the eight concrete batteries, which became part of the U.S. Coast Artillery. From 1944 to 1946, a Veterans' Administration hospital operated at the fort.

People had settled in Prince George's County because of its proximity to the capital, but on the whole, they were a small percentage of the population. As the 19th century drew to a close, however, the city of Washington grew larger and larger, until it spread into Prince George's County. Farming remained a way of life for many in the vast rural areas beyond these new towns, but year by year, the percentage of the population earning their livelihood through agriculture declined as the denser suburban population close to Washington grew.

During World War II, Fort Washington served as the home of the Officer Candidate School of the Adjutant General's Corps. In 1946, the fort was turned over to the Department of Interior for use as a national park. Residents of the Fort Washington region sought industry and commercial enterprise that would assume a life of its own in Prince George's County and transform the county from a bedroom suburb into an equal partner in a dynamic metropolitan area. The challenge of that search is as formidable, adventuresome, and exciting as the taming of the frontier so many years ago.

Fort Washington, one of the most popular areas in Prince George's County, has a rich and vibrant history. The Fort Washington communities including and surrounding the fort are Accokeek, Broad Creek, Chapel Hill, Fort Foote, Friendly, Oxon Hill, Oxon Hill Cove, Piscataway, Silesia, and Tantallon. Fort Washington is now a 341-acre park that offers an array of recreational facilities, including picnic grounds overlooking the Potomac River, fishing, three-and-a-half miles of bike and hiking trails, concerts, reenactments, and playgrounds for children. What had been a county of 30,000 in 1900 became a county of 60,000 in 1930. By 1950, there were almost 200,000 people living in Prince George's County. According to the 1960 census, there were 350,000, and in 1970, the population had grown to more than 661,000. The explosive growth seemed to come to an end, as the next 10 years saw a small decline.

One

PISCATAWAY

The first inhabitants of Piscataway were Native Americans who lived and hunted the lands for more than 200 years. In 1662, more than 3,000 acres were surveyed by order of Lord Baltimore for future settlement. Piscataway was once the name of Maryland along the Potomac north of Mattowoman Creek, including what is now the District of Columbia. The creek runs south for five miles over a plateau with an average elevation of 200 feet. In 1670, Charles County was subdivided, and the western part north of Mattowoman Creek became Piscataway Hundred. As defined by Kathleen A. Kellock, a hundred was an electoral and fiscal district with a constable responsible for the collection of poll taxes. Europeans referred to the land near the creek as Piscataway. The name was retained until 1698, when the settlers along the eastern branch and Rock Creek demanded a separate unit for themselves. Old Piscataway Hundred was then lopped off north of Oxon Run to form New Scotland Hundred.

The National Park Service, of the U.S. Department of the Interior, owns and operates Fort Washington National Park. The 341-acre park offers an assortment of recreational opportunities. The community uses picnic areas, fishes, hikes, rides the biking trials, and plays on the playgrounds. It is not unusual to see eagles circling the river or deer feeding in the park during morning and evening twilight. Over 200 years of army presence has left the park with a diverse group of military structures and a rich history of service to our country and the nation's capital. (Courtesy the Thomas Collection.)

Two

COLONIAL FORT WASHINGTON

In 1608, the British influence began with John Smith's first expedition to the new world. The first settlers came to Prince George's County from the south, leaving the older settlements of Southern Maryland behind to move to new lands farther up the Patuxent and Potomac Rivers. Those pioneers of the 1660s, 1670s, and 1680s came up the rivers by boats and canoes and built simple frame cottages and houses. Life was not easy for the first generation of the settlers. Plantations were not the elegant country seats of legend. Tobacco fields were little more than tiny clearings in the forest. The settlers did not have doctors, churches, clubs, markets, newspapers, schools, or theaters. There was little organized community life. The only links to the outside world were the landings on the riverbanks where they met ships from England that came to collect tobacco and trade goods.

Year by year, more settlers came, and in a generation's time, the banks of the Patuxent and Potomac were lined with homes, farms, and families. By the time Prince George's County was established, there were already 10 other counties in Maryland, five on each shore of the Chesapeake Bay.

In the 18th century, the Fort Washington region grew. The land was settled, and the frontier became a civilization. Settlers—freemen from all parts of the British Isles as well as other countries of Europe—came to find homes here. In addition, Africans were brought to the colonies by way of the West Indies to work as slaves. As the years went by, trading centers along the rivers grew into towns such as Bladensburg, Marlborough, Nottingham, Queen Anne, and Piscataway. Merchants built stores, lawyers and doctors established practices, clergymen consecrated churches, and innkeepers opened their doors to travelers and residents alike. Some iron was even mined and worked in the upper Patuxent region, but the region, despite its growth, remained predominantly agricultural. Agriculture was the basis of the economy and directly or indirectly provided the livelihood for every resident. Tobacco remained the heart of the agricultural economy.

Tobacco created wealth for the Fort Washington region as well as all the towns and villages of Prince George's County. This one crop contributed more to Fort Washington prosperity than anything else, and it created a prosperous, sophisticated tobacco society, which traded its staple crop with English and Scottish merchants for goods from all over the world.

The photograph depicts a typical Colonial woman in the 16th century. The women performed traditional roles such as preparing and serving food, weaving clothing, and raising and educating children. Colonial women took care of multiple crucial tasks simultaneously. The European woman's role was greatly affected by the importation of slavery. The women who could not afford slave help were often permanently put back into household duties.

Fort Washington Park buildings and grounds are administered by the National Capital Parks–East. The park represents one of the more than 380 parks in the national park system. This historical monument is one of the special places saved by the American people so that all may experience our heritage. The photograph depicts a Sunday outing with military families.

Three

FORT WASHINGTON

The history of Fort Washington, Maryland—both the region and the fort—began in the late 18th century. On March 30, 1794, Congress authorized its first series of defensive programs planned to protect the harbors of major cities. George Washington urged that a fort be built at Digges Point, but nothing was done. During the first decades of the 19th century, America depended heavily on coastal fortifications and built forts designed to provide a deterrent to attack by the French and English armies. In June 1807, Congress authorized a new second defense system and appropriated $3 million for a building program. In 1805, while the second fortification system was still being contemplated, a fort was approved by Congress. The fort, Fort Warburton, was completed in 1809. The Digges family owned Warburton Manor, Frankland, and the surrounding tracts of land at that time. The fort stood directly across the river from Mount Vernon, Virginia, the home of George Washington. Gen. George Washington was known to have crossed the Potomac to attend the Broad Creek Church and to occasionally have dinner with Col. William Digges and other families who resided in the Fort Washington area.

On August 27, 1814, Capt. Samuel T. Dyson ordered his garrison to destroy Fort Warburton because they could not defend it against the incursion of a British naval squadron coming upstream to attack the capital. Maj. Pierre L'Enfant and Lt. Col. Walker K. Armistead were commissioned by the government to clear the remains of the old fort and build the new fort. Major L'Enfant and Lieutenant Colonel Armistead, chief engineer of the Alexandria District, were instrumental in the design and building of the new fort, renamed Fort Washington. Construction on Fort Washington started on February 27, 1816, and was completed in 1824. The fort was relocated from Digges Point to its current location on a bluff overlooking the east bank of the Potomac River in Prince George's County, Maryland. The new site was considered an ideal location because of its natural defenses, surrounded by Swann Creek to the north, the Potomac River to the west, and Piscataway Creek to the south. Fort Washington defended the Potomac River and the city of Washington. The materials used to build the new fort included cast-mated brick and stone fortification with earthen outworks—basic elements of American fortifications during the early 19th century.

In 1872, the U.S. Army Corps of Engineers began to prepare a new coastal defense system on the fort's artillery. Between 1873 and 1875, construction on four 15-inch Rodman guns and a magazine were started. At that time, new gun positions were begun, but construction stopped when funds ceased to be received. This 24-pound cannon is all that remains from Fort Washington's 1881 armament. (Courtesy the Thomas Collection.)

Decatur Battery is one of modern fortifications with two 10-inch disappearing gun carriages. The guns were being dismantled to send to the World War I battlefront in Europe, but the Armistice was signed before they were sent overseas. They had not been dismantled at the time of this photograph. (Courtesy National Archives and Records Administration.)

Col. William E. Ellis was coast defense commander of Fort Washington and Fort Hunt. The fort provided housing for officers and enlisted personnel. As indicated in this photograph, housing was well constructed. (Courtesy National Archives and Records Administration.)

X69408

Fort Washington and the Potomac River waterfront are seen in a view from the Fort Hunt wharf. At right are the walls of the old fort. The water towers can also be seen. In 1921, the post was no longer needed. Fort Washington became headquarters for the 12th Infantry. During World War II, the Adjutant General's Officer Candidate School was located at the post. In 1946, the fort was deactivated and became part of the national park system. (Courtesy National Archives and Records Administration.)

Housing and general services were provided for military personnel. At left is the Administration Building, Coast Defense Headquarters. The two buildings at the center and right are company barracks. The water tanks furnished Fort Washington with water for consumption and firefighting. (Courtesy National Archives and Records Administration.)

At left in this April 29, 1919, photograph is the bachelor officer quarters, and to the right are smaller individual buildings that were occupied by married officers. There are many war-era historical portrayals throughout Fort Washington's many living history programs. The commanding officer's quarters, now the visitor's center, was completed in 1822. It served as the home for fort commanders through the 19th century. (Courtesy National Archives and Records Administration.)

This building represents significant administrative activity at the fort. In 1939, Fort Washington was transferred from the War Department to the Department of the Interior. The Adjutant General's Officer Candidate School moved to Fort Washington in January 1942. After Pearl Harbor, the fort reverted back to the War Department. It was later transferred to the Veterans' Administration. In 1946, the fort was returned to the Department of the Interior. (Courtesy National Park Service.)

The quartermaster bakery prepared food at the fort. The bakery was originally a casemate, but gun mounts were never installed. This facility was used to bake bread goods for the soldiers at Fort Washington and Fort Hunt, just across the Potomac River from Fort Washington. The National Park Service installed an iron fence to prevent the octagonal bricks from being stolen or vandalized. (Courtesy National Archives and Records Administration.)

Horse shows and games often entertained the soldiers. During World War I, Fort Washington was garrisoned by the District of Columbia Coast Artillery, and a number of military units were organized at the post. The fort was also used as a staging area for troops going overseas, bringing a constant transition in and out of Fort Washington. This picture, taken by Cpl. P. Boyden, portrays the enlisted men's riding competition. (Courtesy National Archives and Records Administration.)

Frequent competitive activities at the fort offered many gatherings for the soldiers and their wives. There were many car races, equestrian shows, and various competitions. This photograph, taken by Pvt. F. W. King on July 30, 1920, depicts a field meet for a vehicle and horse show. (Courtesy National Archives and Records Administration.)

Fort Washington officers took part in events as judges or contestants; these officers are, from left to right, Col. W. E. Ellis, Col. R. A. McBride, Maj. E. B. Gray, Capt. E. M. Goolrick, Capt. L. C. Mitchell, Lt. A. Crum, Lt. (jg) C. Saylor, Lt. ? LaMarre, Lt. C. M. Meyers, and Lt. H. H. Wilson. Private Horydczak took this picture on April 1, 1920. (Courtesy National Archives and Records Administration.)

During the period from April 1891 to September 1902, fortifications guarding the river approaches were built and existing ones strengthened. Gun batteries were set up across the Potomac River at Fort Hunt. Fort Washington became headquarters for these installations. In 1896, two magazines and gun mounts at the old fort were completed. Fort Washington was garrisoned by Company A, 4th Artillery, the first permanent garrison since 1872. Visitors can now take time out to view the barracks and cannons. (Courtesy National Park Service.)

The 3rd Calvary Band musicians share a history of more than 225 years entertaining servicemen, dating back to the American Revolution. The band has always been an important part of military service and gives talented musicians a unique opportunity to do what they do best—play music. The 3rd Calvary Band was assigned to the Fort Washington garrison, providing musical entertainment and boosting soldiers' morale, entertaining civilians, and assisting with military ceremonies. (Courtesy National Park Service.)

In 1845, $6,000 was requested to construct a hospital, but funding was not approved. The first approved hospital was a 12-bed building near the main gate. In 1904, the surgeon general approved plans to increase the hospital capacity to 30 patients. Prior to the building of the hospital, soldiers died from disease more than from enemy bullets. A Sergeant Combs photographed this scene on April 29, 1919. (Courtesy National Archives and Records Administration.)

In 1896, eight concrete batteries were positioned near the old fort. Endicott-era guns (c. 1887, when Secretary of War William C. Endicott recommend a new system of seacoast defense) were outfitted, consisting of 10-inch rifles on disappearing carriages, 12-inch mortar batteries, and 4-inch rifles. In 1898, after the Spanish-American War, mines were removed from the Potomac River, and later that year, the 10-inch gun mounted near Battery Humphreys was moved to a new mount. (Courtesy National Archives and Records Administration.)

Battery Emory, started in 1896, mounted two 10-inch guns. Battery Decatur was started in 1891 and mounted two 10-inch guns. Battery Humphreys, started in 1898, also mounted two 10-inch guns. Battery White was started in 1899 and mounted two 4-inch guns. In July 1899, Batteries Emory, Decatur, Humphreys, and White were officially under the artillery commander of the fort. Sergeant Combs took this photograph on April 29, 1919. (Courtesy National Archives and Records Administration.)

The Fort Washington Visitor's Center is located in a house at the top of the hill on the park's grounds. The visitor's center houses exhibits on the history of the fort. The park service provides an audiovisual program and an exploration of the park's history. The gift shop contains books, postcards, and other materials related to the wars and the history of the fort. (Courtesy the Thomas Collection.)

Built in 1857, the first light tower at Fort Washington was an 18.5-foot iron post until the 1870s. Early lighthouses burned whale oil in metal lamps, and later lamps had mirror-like reflectors. In 1946, the light station was under control of the U.S. Coast Guard. Light keepers left the fort in 1984. The light went to an unmanned, automatic flashing red light. Light 80 is still operated by the Coast Guard. (Courtesy National Park Service.)

Fort Washington

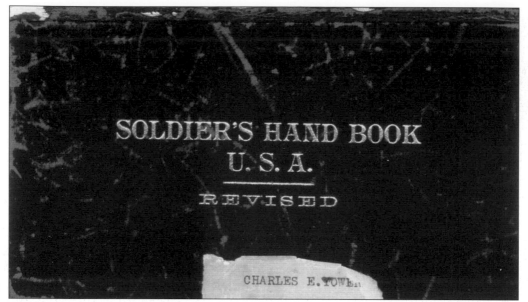

SOLDIER'S HAND BOOK
U.S.A.
REVISED

CHARLES E. YOWELL

The pictured image is the *Soldier's Hand Book*. Soldiers assigned to Fort Washington all received individual handbooks that outlined the fort's mission; information on training and uniforms; information on buildings such as the hospital, the mess hall, and exercise rooms; and rules and regulations. The book was designed to orient the new soldier to his surroundings and service within the U.S. Army. (Courtesy National Park Service.)

Fort Washington was part of the harbor defenses of Washington, D.C. In 1809, Fort Warburton was constructed to protect the perimeter of the nation's capital against the British. A counterscarp battery—the outer slope or wall of a ditch or moat in a fortification—was constructed to protect the right wall of the fortress. (Courtesy National Park Service.)

The mining casemate was protected from enemy attack by 15 feet of earth and contained the switchboard used to fire the mines. The mines can be exploded individually or in groups. Fort Washington's first mining casemate was in a ravine about 700 yards north of the old fort. Work began in 1890, and the structure was completed by 1892. In 1906, a new casemate was built in the courtyard of the fort's southwest demibastion, and the south casemates were filled to protect the structure from enemy gunfire. (Courtesy the Woods Collection.)

Battery Decatur, formerly known as Emplacement B, was changed to its present name by General Order 43, dated April 4, 1900. Battery Decatur is named in honor of Commo. Stephen N. Decatur, a native of Maryland who served with distinction during the war with Tripoli and the War of 1812. Battery Decatur was armed with two Model 1888 breech-loading rifles on disappearing carriages. Over 30 feet long, these guns weighed 67,200 pounds and used smokeless powder to fire a 75-pound shell six-and-a-half miles. (Courtesy the Thomas Collection.)

Clothing account of *Charles G. Tower*
Co. "H", 4th Regiment *Artillery*

MONEY ALLOWANCE FOR CLOTHING.

(Note.—First sergeants will enter the amount allowed opposite each year after the annual price list is received.)

For the 1st year .... $ ---------
" 2d year .... ---------
" 3d year .... ---------
Total for 3 years .... $ ---------

CLOTHING RECEIVED.

When received.	Articles.	Price.		Due soldier at settlement.		Due U. S. at settlement.	
		Dolls.	Cts.	Dolls.	Cts.	Dolls.	Cts.
Aug. 3. 1898	1 For Cap		74				
	1 Ornament		16				
	2 B Shirts	3	90				
	2 Un. Shirts		80				
	1 C Shoes	2	23				
	4 Socks		24				
	1 Blouse	4	41				
	1 Blanket	3	83				

Clothing received—Continued.

When received.	Articles.	Price.		Due soldier at settlement.		Due U. S. at settlement.	
		Dolls.	Cts.	Dolls.	Cts.	Dolls.	Cts.
	1 Cam. Hat.		85				
	1 Leggins		64				
	2 Un Shirts		58				
	4 Collars		16				
	2 Drawers		80				
Aug 18-98	1 Drawers		40				
" 24-98	1 Un. Trousers	2	00				
	1 Un Shirt		40				
	1 C Coat.		98				
	1 C Trousers		73				
Sept 29-98	1 Ornament		15				

Every article of equipment except for arms and accoutrements belonging to the regiment is marked with the number and name of the regiment. This account includes camp and garrison equipment for cavalry men stationed at Fort Washington. A record is kept of all issues and purchases to the soldiers in federal records. (Courtesy National Archives and Records Administration.)

This uniformed soldier is photographed in full dress by a professional photographer. He probably sent the picture home to his family. The unidentified soldier is authentically dressed in the U.S. Army uniform. The fort offers living history presentations for public viewing, where National park historians and volunteers dressed in authentic uniforms recreate the life of a 19th-century garrison. (Courtesy National Park Service.)

Guard House

When ocean-going warships were made of wood and carried smoothbore cannons, no enemy would attempt to ascend the river before destroying the fort; however, changing technology made the fort useless. The government built concrete emplacements to meet the threat of iron-sided ships and rifled guns. When the emplacements became obsolete, the post was turned over to the infantry and finally became a military training facility. Over 200 years of army presence has left the park with a diverse group of military structures and a rich history of service to the country and the nation's capital. (Courtesy National Park Service.)

Fort Washington Hospital Corps medical personnel includes nurses, orderlies, and doctors trained to treat sick and wounded soldiers. Medical service includes providing triage, first aid, and immunizations as needed during war and peacetime. The hospital situation at Fort Washington can be considered typical of army posts. In 1835, an army medical board examined all the military forts and stations and found only three well-built army hospitals. (Courtesy National Park Service.)

The British attack on and subsequent burning of Washington, D.C., powerfully showed a new defensive plan was needed. The Fort Washington that we know today began to take form during the wake of the War of 1812. Armored ships were able to approach closer than wooden ships and could use rifled cannons to demolish brick fortifications. (Courtesy the Thomas Collection.)

Between 1896 and 1921, many buildings were erected as living quarters on the grounds of Fort Washington. Many Victorian houses lined the parade ground, including bachelor officers' and non-commissioned officers' living quarters and other support structures. This non-commissioned officers' duplex was built in 1909.

The lighthouse is located at the bottom of a steep hill leading to the Potomac River and is used as a channel marker. A trip to the lighthouse covers a winding, tree-lined road featuring a scenic view of the Potomac River. The area is utilized as a public park where people picnic and fish. (Courtesy National Park Service.)

Visitors enjoy a view of the Potomac River from the fort. Besides historical facts, many fun things happen on the Potomac River. People enjoy canoeing, riding the ferry, whitewater rafting, hiking, and fishing. There are many historical sites along the river, including the Jefferson and Lincoln Memorials, the Lyndon B. Johnson Park, and the Washington Monument. (Courtesy National Park Service.)

In 1896, the only buildings at the fort were the commandant's house, the fort, and the small building down the hill from the house. The officers' row was built between 1896 and 1921. Victorian houses lined the parade ground. (Courtesy National Park Service.)

Antietam and Manassas were fought within a cannon's roar of the Potomac River. The Potomac River starts in West Virginia and plunges 281 miles to meet tidal water at the District of Columbia line. The 101-mile-long lower river is broad and stately, 11 miles wide at its mouth. Capt. John Smith is credited with being the first European to explore the "Potowmack River" in 1608. Thomas Jefferson referred to the river as "one of the most stupendous scenes in nature."

The early barracks were designed and arranged in a quadrangle. In 1903, the 104th Company of Coast Artillery was assigned to serve the new rapid-fire batteries at the Fort Washington garrison. Each company was assigned its own barracks. The other units were the 44th, 117th, and 37th Companies. (Courtesy National Archives and Records Administration.)

The following information was told by Carolyn Ritch, the wife of Jack Ritch. In the mid-1950s, Charles Ortman and Jack Ritch built a modern rest station at the lower level of the hill in the fort. The Ritch family and associates worked on the construction of the station. The family has lived in the vicinity of the park ever since and visited there many times over the years, having picnics and exploring the forts. (Courtesy the Woods Collection.)

The old fort sits on the high ground overlooking the Potomac River. It offers a scenic view of Washington, D.C., and the shoreline of Virginia. Only one silent gun stands behind the masonry wall that once sheltered the strong armament of a powerful fort protecting and guarding the waters of the nation's capital. (Courtesy National Park Service.)

Raising the flag daily symbolizes the love and pride of nation and is a poignant reminder of America's greatness and the fortune of citizens to live in a country that values freedom above all else. It signifies the commitment made by fallen comrades who battled bravely to defend the honor of this sacred land representing American unity, power, and purpose as a nation, and it exemplifies the devotion of leaders who continue to uphold its promise of liberty, justice, and freedom for all. (Courtesy the Thomas Collection.)

This was the first modern artillery position built for the defense of Washington. Battery Decatur is named in honor of Commo. Stephen N. Decatur, a native of Maryland. Battery Decatur's structures include the battery commander's station and lower parade behind the battery. The commander's station houses the instruments for directing the two guns at Battery Decatur.

The Fort Washington Quartermaster's Store supplied the fort all supplies necessary to outfit a soldier on the battlefield. Quartermasters provide a host of supply and service functions and experiment with new modes of transportation. It was the quartermaster's responsibility to transport unprecedented levels of supplies and personnel. In 1862, the Quartermaster Department assumed responsibility for burial of war dead. Quartermasters have served as teamsters, launderers, typewriter specialists, shoe repairmen, depot operators, and paymasters. They are also responsible for training. (Courtesy National Park Service.)

In 1881, several captains and pilots petitioned the Lighthouse Board for a fog bell to be placed at Fort Washington. This was approved, and a tower was built in 1882 to house the fog bell. The fog bell tower would rise to a height of 32 feet, with a base of 16 feet narrowing to 4 feet at the top. The bell rang once every 15 seconds. (Courtesy National Park Service.)

In 1909, builders constructed non-commissioned officer (NCO) quarters to house the two NCOs and their families. Non-commissioned staff quarters were also built and completed in 1922. They were designated as homes for senior sergeants of the post. (Courtesy National Park Service.)

Both officers and non-commissioned officers required living and sleeping quarters at the fort. The commanding officer's quarters, presently the visitor's center, was completed in 1822. It served as a home for the fort commander through the 19th century. (Courtesy National Park Service.)

In 1899, after the navy destroyed the Spanish fleet at Santiago, Cuba, the Spanish-American War was over. The mines were removed from the Potomac River. During World War I, the guns of Battery Decatur were removed and shipped to Fort Monroe, Virginia, at which time they were shipped to Europe for use in France. (Courtesy National Park Service.)

This picture depicts an entrance referred to as a "sally port." A sally port is a gate or passage into a fortified place. Sally raids—raids launched from sally ports—attempted to slow the offensive siege process. Targets for the raids included tools that could be captured and used by the defenders, labor-intensive works such as trenches and mines, and siege engines and siege towers. In addition, enemy laborers were also targeted. (Courtesy National Park Service.)

Officers, and later enlisted men, used these living quarters. Standardized plans designed for the Army Housing Program were based on historic architectural styles that reflected a region's history and local building materials. At posts on the Atlantic seaboard, buildings were designed in the quartermaster's version of the Colonial style; construction in the Southwest was based on Spanish Mission architecture. (Courtesy National Park Service.)

This building served the heart of the fort, where the day-to-day management plans were planned and put into action. Administrative and military personnel were trained at Fort Washington. In 1939, Fort Washington was transferred from the War Department to the Department of the Interior. The Adjutant General's Officer Candidate School moved to Fort Washington in January 1942. (Courtesy National Park Service.)

Picturesque Fort Washington sits on high ground overlooking the Potomac River and offers a grand view of the Washington, D.C., and Virginia shoreline. From this view, a visitor can look right into Mount Vernon, the home of Gen. George Washington, and into Fort Hunt in Alexandria, Virginia. (Courtesy the Thomas Collection.)

In 1946, the fort was deactivated and turned over to the national park system. Under the management of park service, the grounds were opened to the public for tours, picnics, and other recreational activities. The fort continues to preserve the history and provides recreational facilities for the community and visitors. (Courtesy the Thomas Collection.)

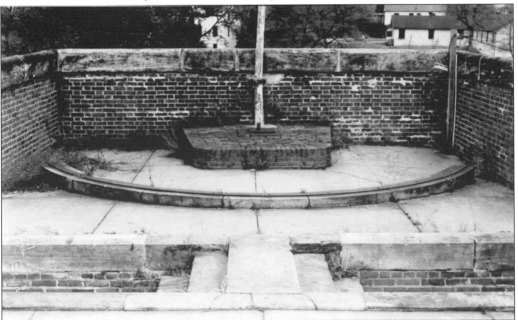

The landscape includes a drawbridge leading to the entrance. Today only one silent gun stands behind the masonry wall, the last armament of a powerful fort that once guarded the water approach to the nation's capital. The old fort is one of the few American seacoast fortifications still in its original form. (Courtesy the Thomas Collection.)

Fort Washington Park offers a great setting for family and organizational picnics. There are tables and grills for small groups throughout the park and available on a first-come, first-serve basis from the time the park opens until dark. It is the responsibility of the citizens as well as the National Park Service group to protect park property; preserve trees, flowers, and all wildlife; and maintain order and keep the area in a clean orderly condition. (Courtesy National Park Service.)

The 104th Cavalry Company was one of the first artillery units to serve Battery Decatur at Fort Washington. A Coast Artillery Company consisted of three officers and about 90 enlisted men who were assigned to serve each 10-inch battery. The company was further divided into a fire control or range section and two gun sections. (Courtesy National Park Service.)

Four

BROAD CREEK

The Broad Creek community is located in the Broad Creek Historic District of Prince George's County. For more than 200 years, Broad Creek has been considered a special place because of its history, natural features, and architectural and archeological resources. Broad Creek has retained its image as a quiet semi-rural enclave separate from the busy commercial and residential development that surrounds it. It is a reminder of Prince George's agrarian heritage, when tobacco raising and shipbuilding were the most important industries in the county. The town of Aire, also known as Broad Creek, was one of the six towns established in Prince George's County in 1706 by the Maryland General Assembly as a port for shipping tobacco.

This sign is a guide for visitors to follow the road to the Broad Creek Historical District. St. John's is a picturesque wooded area containing about five acres of open space. Located in the Broad Creek Historic District, it is bounded by a large stream on one side and Livingston Road on the other. It contains a baseball field used by the local Little League and a playground used by the school. The site is used for annual fairs and other outdoor activities. A variety of small ancillary structures are located around the property. (Courtesy the Thomas Collection.)

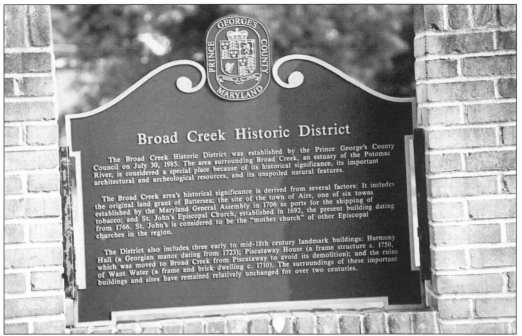

This sign reflects the historical significance of the Broad Creek district. The area was established about 1694. In 1984, the Prince George's Historic Preservation Commission voted to establish a Broad Creek Historic District. On June 30, 1985, the decision was upheld by the Prince George's County Council. (Courtesy the Thomas Collection.)

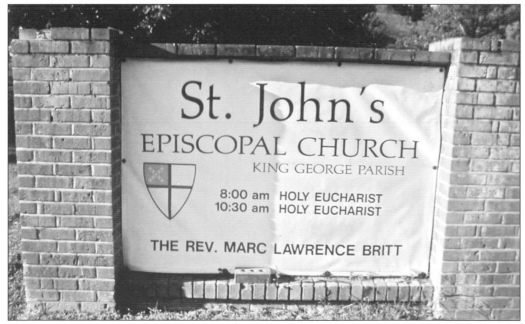

For over two centuries, the historical site for the Broad Creek Church, now officially known as St. John's Episcopal Church, has remained relatively unchanged. In 1692, St John's was one of the first churches established in Maryland. It is the mother church of the Washington Diocese and of other Episcopal churches in the region. (Courtesy St. John's historian Phyllis Cox.)

The Broad Creek Church is the mother church for other Episcopal churches in the region. It is now known as St. John's Episcopal Church; established in 1692, it was one of the first churches in Maryland. The parish of St. John's continues to serve the surrounding communities of Fort Washington and Oxon Hill. (Courtesy the Woods Collection.)

According to one local history, the earliest grave recorded dates from 1760 and is flanked by a rose bush over 100 years old. Many names from the southern part of the county are recorded in the cemetery. Names on plots and headstones include Hatton, Kerby, and Thorne. (Courtesy the Woods Collection.)

The St. John's graveyard in Broad Creek is one of the oldest cemeteries in Prince George's County and has many old stone markers, including those for two soldiers and two patriots of the Revolution. Here lie the remains of the many prominent locals, such as John Addison, James Edelen, and George Athey. (Courtesy the Woods Collection.)

The graveyard contains several hundred grave markers dating from the early 19th century to the present day. Several founding members of the St. John's congregation are buried in the cemetery that encircles the original chapel. Many of the gravesites were placed under the shade of large maple trees. Modern structures and highways serving the Fort Washington community are a few hundred yards away, but the cemetery and its surroundings are quite serene and well maintained. (Courtesy the Thomas Collection.)

St. John's (Broad Creek) Church's entrance is still in its original foundation, with stained-glass windows honoring some of the first families of the parish. The bricks were made on the property. In 1766, the builder was authorized to take down all of the old brick and build a new building. In 1768, this building was completed and still stands. (Courtesy the Woods Collection and *Along the Potomac Shore in Prince George's County*.)

Built in 1696, St. John's (Broad Creek) Church and its archway's design were dictated by the Church of England. Earlier families, visitors, and parishioners, such as the Magruder family and George Washington, passed through the new check entrance. Washington attended services here from time to time after making an easy trip up to the Potomac River and Broad Creek in his multi-oared barge. (Courtesy the Woods Collection.)

Harmony Hall is an 18th-century Georgian country house that architecturally ranks as one of the great early plantation houses and an outstanding early Colonial house of Maryland. The front of the house faces the Potomac River and remains much as it appeared in 1766, the estimated time of construction. (Courtesy HABS, Library of Congress, Prints and Photographs Division.)

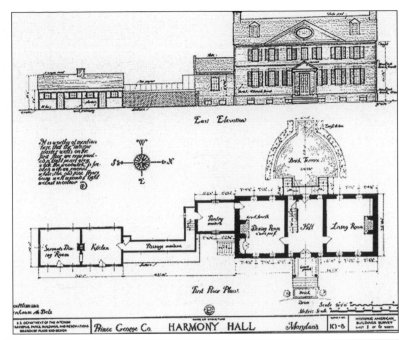

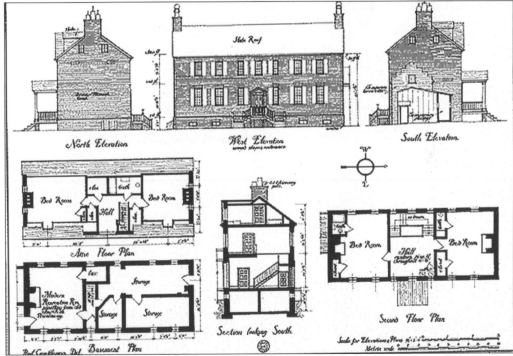

Harmony Hall is located in the Broad Creek Historic District, the first historic district formed under the Prince George's County Preservation Law. This pencil sketch enhanced detailed carpentry and historic restoration of the house. Harmony Hall is an example of Georgian architecture with an I-shaped house plan on a large tract of land also known as Battersea. The home was constructed in the mid-18th century by Enoch Magruder. The home remained in the Magruder-Lyles family until 1850. (Courtesy HABS, Library of Congress, Prints and Photographs Division.)

In 1668, the tract of land on which Harmony Hall is now situated was patented under the name of Battersea by an attorney who practiced in the Prince George's County Court. The title of the property passed by wills to prominent families in the area. As described in William Tyler's will, "my own dwelling plantation" indicates the existence of a plantation dwelling house on the property. In 1966, Harmony Hall was acquired by the National Park Service under the provisions of the Capper-Crampton Act of 1930. In 1980, Harmony Hall was placed on the National Register of Historic Places. (Courtesy HABS, Library of Congress, Prints and Photographs Division.)

According to local tradition, the original Harmony Hall building was constructed in 1723. In 1798, Mrs. Walter Delany Addison, the daughter of a celebrated Colonial portrait painter, named the property Harmony Hall. Throughout the years, structural changes were made to Harmony Hall. George Washington, after attending services at the St. John's (Broad Creek) Church, frequently dined at Harmony Hall. (Courtesy HABS, Library of Congress, Prints and Photographs Division.)

For a brief period in 1793 and 1794, the house was rented by two brothers, John and Walter Addison, sons of Col. Thomas Addison, and their brides, who enjoyed the fireplace. Their happy cohabitation inspired the new name, Harmony Hall. In 1929, Harmony Hall and Want Water were purchased by Charles Collins. In 1966, Collins conveyed Harmony Hall and Want Water to the National Park Service. (Courtesy HABS, Library of Congress, Prints and Photographs Division.)

Harmony Hall is a Georgian (1710–1800) building that is symmetrical in plan and façade. It has a gabled or hipped roof, central entrance, dentiled cornice, a full entablature, and generally a center stairway. Harmony Hall includes exceptional interior details such as this graceful stairway, paneled cupboard, and fretwork chair rails. (Courtesy HABS, Library of Congress, Prints and Photographs Division.)

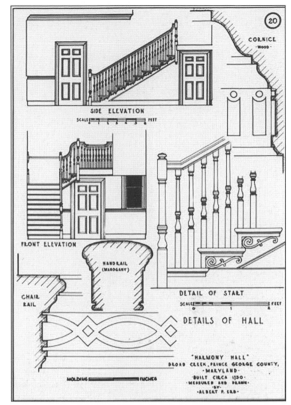

The doors of Harmony Hall represent a classical, symmetrical style of decorative crown and cornices. The panel doors were a favorite style that conveyed a sense of dignity and prestige and served as a reminder of New England to the Georgian home. Only affluent colonists such as the Magruders and Addisons were able to afford the workmanship and detail of those doors. (Courtesy HABS, Library of Congress, Prints and Photographs Division.)

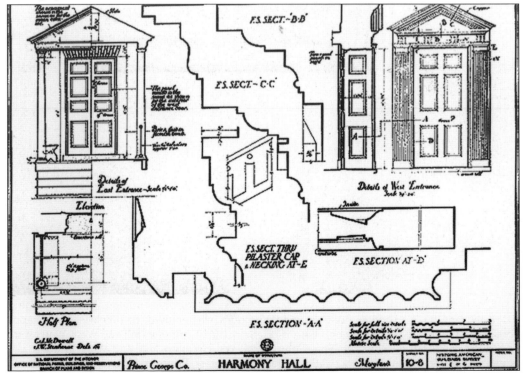

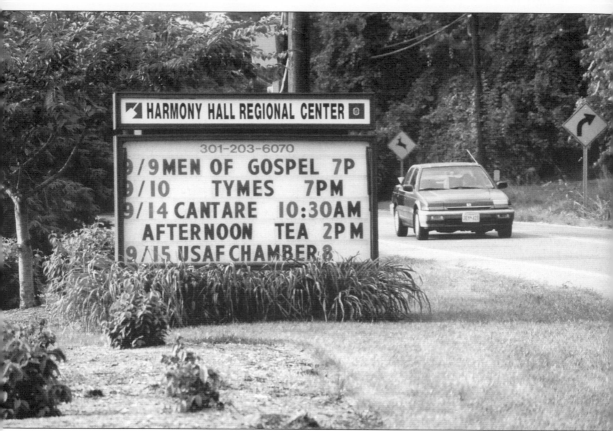

HARMONY HALL REGIONAL CENTER

301-203-6070
9/9 MEN OF GOSPEL 7P
9/10 TYMES 7PM
9/14 CANTARE 10:30AM
AFTERNOON TEA 2PM
9/15 USAF CHAMBER 8

Harmony Hall Regional Center is located on Livingston and Fort Washington Road. The marquee announces upcoming events to be held in the center during the course of the year. The center, located in a converted elementary school formerly known as Harmony Hall Elementary School, provides recreational classes and events geared to the community. (Courtesy the Thomas Collection.)

The Harmony Hall Regional Center facility houses an art and concert hall. The art portion of the facility provides a variety of fine arts programs, including classes in the visual arts, theater, and dance. The John Addison Concert Hall and galleries offer music, dance, and dramatic programs and exhibitions. Natural resources are also highlighted at the center with classes and exhibit space available for those whose interests lie outdoors. In addition, the administrative offices for the Maryland National Capital Parks and Planning Commission are housed in Harmony Hall. (Courtesy the Thomas Collection.)

The community of Battersea on the Bay is named after a 500-acre tract of land now known as Harmony Hall. Battersea, a diverse residential community, borders the Potomac River and Broad Creek. Harmony Hall currently comprises only 65 acres of the original tract. Portions of the tract that were sold off are now occupied by the Harmony Hall Regional Center, Silesia Store, the Washington Suburban Sanitation Commission pumping station, and the Piscataway House. During the Colonial period, Battersea was first known as Batchelour's Harbour because two bachelors had purchased the tract of land located in the Piscataway Hundred in October 1662. Between Batchelour's Harbour and Warburton was a small wedge-shaped tract not patented until 1687. Battersea's shoreline was used as a port for tobacco barges. From the Colonial period to the mid-1940s, the land was used for tobacco farming. Battersea on the Bay is surrounded by many historical sites, such as St. John's Episcopal Church, also known as Broad Creek Church. (Courtesy the Thomas Collection.)

Five

ANTEBELLUM PLANTATIONS

The antebellum homes of Colonial Piscataway show a progressive architectural transition from the Tidewater model to the modern-day two-and-a-half-story Georgian home. The Tidewater home marked a leading style and trend that was affected by regional and international influence. The first pioneer homes built were basic one- or two-room dwellings sufficient for a small family starting out in an agricultural environment. As the wealth of the region grew, people started to add wings on both sides of the house and built even larger brick homes such as Harmony Hall. The basic floor plans included a center hall flanked by a parlor on each side. During the 17th and 18th centuries, the homes were influenced by English architects and were usually one-and-a-half stories with a gabled roof, often a full-width, shed-roof porch, and paneled interiors. The Georgian-style home was classically inspired and was usually a two-story dwelling with a central stair hall. The Belleview, Want Water, and Harmony Hall were characteristic of such building types and styles.

In 1641, William Digges was granted a patent to Warburton Manor, a parcel of land that was originally part of the Dr. Barbier del Barbier estate. Lying at a great bend of the Potomac, it afforded the Digges family a magnificent view upriver and southwestward toward the Virginia shore. The Digges house faced George Washington's Mount Vernon from the head of a long formal garden at the mouth of the Piscataway Creek near Marshall Hall. According to legend, signals were exchanged between William Digges and George Washington when visits were planned. One road from the house led down to the landing on the Potomac, where visitors came ashore and the tobacco and wheat of Warburton Manor were loaded for shipment. Another road went down to a bridge or ferry to the Little Piscattaway (original spelling) Town passing through the Hatton estate. A third road went off northeastward to the Digges Mill, the Calverts' Mount Airy, Stephen West's Woodyard, Ignatius Digges's Melwood, and the county seat, Upper Marlborough. (Courtesy the Miles Collection.)

Around 1840, Belleview Plantation, also known as the Steed House, was built by Enoch Magruder. Belleview is a Greek Revival plantation house, one of the few surviving examples in Prince George's County of a style typical of successful small plantations of the period. In 1856, the property was conveyed to Lenora Lowe and her husband, James M. Steed, who enlarged the house. Belleview remained the Steed family home until the late 1960s. (Courtesy HABS, Library of Congress, Prints and Photographs Division.)

Belleview Plantation, seen from the southeast, is one of the—if not the—oldest dwellings remaining in the Broad Creek Historic District. The house, as it stands today without the wings, is in external form exactly the same as when it was first built. According to tradition, the house may have been constructed in the late 17th century or early 18th century, shortly after Col. Thomas Addison received the patent. (Courtesy HABS, Library of Congress, Prints and Photographs Division.)

In 1760, Enoch Magruder purchased Belleview, Harmony Hall, and Mount Lubentia. Belleview became the home of his grandson, Lloyd M. Lowe, who inherited the property in 1798. Lowe enlarged the house, doubling its depth with the addition of a rear stair hall and flanking parlor, raising the roof, and adding dormers. The photograph shows a general view of the southeast and northeast elevations. (Courtesy HABS, Library of Congress, Prints and Photographs Division.)

Belleview's northeast elevation, in the architectural tradition of the southern Tidewater region, began as a modest hall-and-parlor-plan house about 1792. The house underwent a number of modifications around 1830, evolving into a more sophisticated dwelling with fine Greek Revival moldings and mantels. The current house has a one-and-a-half-story side-gabled main block with an addition plus a one-story kitchen addition with a loft. (Courtesy HABS, Library of Congress, Prints and Photographs Division.)

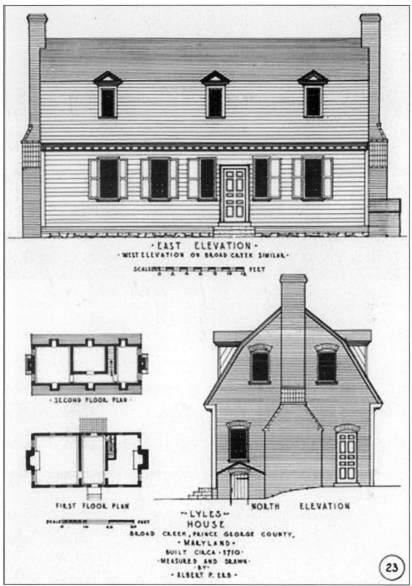

· EAST ELEVATION ·
· WEST ELEVATION ON BROAD CREEK SIMILAR ·

SCALING _____ FEET

· SECOND FLOOR PLAN ·

FIRST FLOOR PLAN

SCALE _____ FEET

· LYLES ·
HOUSE

NORTH ELEVATION

BROAD CREEK, PRINCE GEORGE COUNTY,
· MARYLAND ·
BUILT CIRCA · 1710 ·
· MEASURED AND DRAWN ·
· BY ·
· ALBERT P. ELS ·

(23)

Want Water, the Lyles house, also may be the oldest dwelling remaining in the vicinity of Fort Washington. According to tradition, the house may have been constructed in the late 17th century or early 18th century, shortly after Col. Thomas Addison received the patent. Want Water, as originally patented, was a long, narrow strip of land that embraced almost all of the east bank of Church Branch of Broad Creek. Upon the death of Colonel Addison in 1727, Want Water went to his oldest son, John, who later conveyed it to Humphrey Batt by deed in November 1736. After the Addisons disposed of Want Water in 1736, the most prominent owner was Col. William Lyles, a wealthy landowner and son-in-law of Enoch Magruder. He lived here at the time of the Revolution, then he moved to Alexandria, where he was a stockholder in Farmers Bank of Alexandria. Colonel Lyles was an intimate friend of George Washington. Washington frequently passed the very doors of Want Water to worship at Broad Creek Church and occasionally stopped for dinner with his friends at Want Water. (Courtesy HABS, Library of Congress, Prints and Photographs Division.)

Want Water

Want Water is located in the Broad Creek Historic District. In 1756, Batt deeded Want Water to his son-in-law, Richard Barnes. Barnes conveyed his deed to Enoch Magruder in 1761. Upon Magruder's death, it went to his elder daughter, Sarah, the wife of Colonel Lyles. The house, as it stands today without the wings, is in external form exactly the same as when it was originally built. (Courtesy HABS, Library of Congress, Prints and Photographs Division.)

Today the only remains of the original house are two end brick walls with chimneys and fieldstone foundations. As a framed structure, it was not properly maintained by the owners. Therefore, it was allowed to decay and deteriorate. The building is still standing; however, it is in ruins. (Courtesy HABS, Library of Congress, Prints and Photographs Division.)

Want Water's ruins present significant information about the construction techniques and architecture of a Tidewater home of that period. Want Water was considered unusual in its substantial construction, fine details, and its center-hall plan. This picture of the ruins was photographed by the Historic American Buildings Survey (HABS) in 1936. Want Water was built for Col. Thomas Addison, the first county surveyor, soon after 1706–1707. (Courtesy HABS, Library of Congress, Prints and Photographs Division.)

St. James Hill, a two-story house, is located on Livingston Road southwest of Piscataway. Capt. James Neale had the land surveyed between 1661 and 1663. In 1681, he deeded it to his son, James Jr., and daughter-in-law, Elizabeth Calvert, as a wedding present. They later purchased a home in Port Tobacco and sold the land to Giles Blizzard of London. Giles and Mary Blizzard lived at St. James until their daughter, Ann, married Rev. John Fraser in 1710. (Courtesy HABS, Library of Congress, Prints and Photographs Division.)

This view of St. James from the southeast was taken on April 14, 1936, by John O. Brostrup, a surveyor, around the time Lorena Boswell and her brother H. Curly Boswell purchased and restored St. James. The Boswell family used the home and land as a summer retreat, but it was left vacant a lot of the time and again fell to decay and vandalism. (Courtesy HABS, Library of Congress, Prints and Photographs Division.)

St. James is seen from the front with a wing on the right. The house was a classical Georgian home of southern Maryland with a central hallway and two parlors located on either side, one used as a parlor and the other as the family room. The bedrooms were upstairs. It is assumed that the added wing houses the kitchen, which, due to the frequency of fires, was often away from the main house. (Courtesy HABS, Library of Congress, Prints and Photographs Division.)

According to the deeds on file, the St. James land was divided and owned by the Frasers, Bowies, and Thomas Mundel before it was sold to Dr. Benedict Joseph Semmes in 1834. After the death of her father, Dr. Semmes, Celestia Semmes sold the property to Joseph and Annie Hostetter of Lancaster County, Pennsylvania, on November 16, 1869. (Courtesy HABS, Library of Congress, Prints and Photographs Division.)

William Hatton owned Hatton Mansion. Hatton Mansion, formerly known as Batchelour's Harbour, was originally part of an 800-acre tract owned by Jeremiah Dickeson and Stephen Montague. In 1667, Dickinson sold his interest to Montague for 3,300 pounds of tobacco. In 1670, Montague sold Batchelour's Harbour to Hugh French for 10,000 pounds of tobacco. In 1663, French renamed his tract Hatton Point for William Hatton, who transported Mr. French to Maryland. (Courtesy HABS, Library of Congress, Prints and Photographs Division.)

This view of Hatton Mansion from the northwest (front) shows the house beginning to collapse through decay and neglect. The roof of the porch was already falling down. The wood was splintering from the elements and ravages of time. This photograph was taken by John O. Brostrup (of HABS) on May 12, 1936. It was already too late for preservationists to save this beautiful house. (Courtesy HABS, Library of Congress, Prints and Photographs Division.)

This east view of Hatton Mansion illustrates the famous double chimney that was used for both heating and cooking. The house foundation was wooden, and due to time and neglect, the house became unsafe for human occupancy. (Courtesy HABS, Library of Congress, Prints and Photographs Division.)

Hatton Mansion was the main house on an 800-acre tract of prime land near Warburton Manor. It was originally patented by William Hatton and remained in the Hatton family until a fire in 1857. Old Hatton Mansion was a two-story Georgian building with two chimneys. The double-chimney house was larger and more comfortable for its 18th-century inhabitants than the center-chimney type. The house was built during the 18th and early 19th centuries. The original Hatton Mansion was owned by many prominent families through a succession of marriages.

Six

CHAPEL HILL COMMUNITY

Chapel Hill, a post–Civil War African American farming community, began with the establishment of a Freedmen's Bureau school and a Methodist meetinghouse. According to the 1830 census, the settlement and landownership consisted of free blacks. The area grew along the intersection of old roads connecting Fort Washington, Fort Foote, and Piscataway. Before the Civil War, the land was part of the plantations of the Hatton, Edelen, Thorne, and Gallahan families, located on tracts known as Boarman's Content and Frankland. By the 1880s, several families of free blacks and freedmen began to settle and establish small farms on tracts of land purchased from former plantation owners. In October 1868, the Johnson Hill School was built with materials and aid from the Bureau of Freedman's Refugees, Freedmen and Abandoned Lands. The school was presumably named after Charles Johnson, an active trustee of the school during Reconstruction. Mary A. Davinger, a black woman from Philadelphia, was the first teacher (1868–1869). Thomas G. Douglas followed Ms. Davinger as the teacher hired by the bureau.

By 1905, several African American families, including the Hensons, Colberts, Brooks, Hawkins, and Delaneys, had settled in the Chapel Hill area. As the children married, built homes, and raised their own families, they built a benevolent society lodge offering a meeting place and emergency support for the members. Childhood memories in Chapel Hill reflect a strong, stable community of closely related families who took care of one another and were largely self-sufficient. In 1927, the new Livingston Road was constructed along the southern edge of Chapel Hill, providing a direct route southeast from Broad Creek on the Potomac to the village of Piscataway. In the 1930s, the Chapel Hill community included 35 houses, several general stores, a church and two connected schoolhouses, and the benevolent society lodge.

Several commercial establishments have been constructed along Livingston Road. Older houses have been replaced by new ones, and several new residential subdivisions have been built along Old Fort Road. Reminders of the old community are harder to find, but archival records and the recollections of those families make it possible to get a glimpse of Chapel Hill. Though some of the historic properties are no longer standing, the community included Grace Methodist Episcopal Church and cemetery, Chapel Hill School, the Albert Owen Shorter House, the Charles Ball House, the Lancaster House, and the Colbert House.

The Chapel Hill sign points to an early post–Civil War African American farming community located near the intersection of old roads connecting Fort Washington, Fort Foote, and the village of Piscataway. In 1868, Chapel Hill was started with the establishment of a Freedmen's Bureau school and Methodist meetinghouse. The families included the Hensons, Colberts, Brooks, Hawkins, and Delaneys, who were either former slaves of the original plantation owners or freedmen. (Courtesy the Thomas Collection.)

In 1868, Albert Owen Shorter built the Shorter House. Shorter was a freedman who purchased land from the Hattons. Shorter built this two-story, side-gabled, Foxwood frame home. The house entrance was in the central bay of a three-bay main façade. Mr. Shorter was a community leader who helped established the Chapel Hill community, school, and Grace Methodist Church. Descendants of the Shorter family still reside in the Fort Washington area.

On March 12, 1870, seven church trustees purchased a one-and-a-half-acre plot of land from Matilda Sansbury and formed the Providence United Methodist Episcopal Church South. A small church cemetery is maintained at the original site on Old Fort Road. Family members built the church under the leadership of William H. Adams. In 1901, the church relocated to the Friendly settlement at 10700 Old Fort Road. Samuel M. and Mary Sorels donated land on June 21, 1901. (Courtesy the Providence United Methodist Web page [http://provumeth. homestead.com/] and the Thomas Collection.)

GRACE United Methodist Church
CHURCH SCHOOL   WORSHIP   WED. BIBLE STUDY
9:30 AM   8:00 AM & 10:45 AM   7:30 PM
9/10 MOVIE NIGHT 5 PM
17 WOMEN OF GLORY WORSHIP 3 PM
30 ABSTINENCE TILL MARRIAGE
WORKSHOP 5 PM
Rev. Dr. Diana Parker, Associate
NO PARKING HERE TO CORNER

Behind the sign, the Grace Methodist Church has an enormous history. Between 1880 and 1883, the first Methodist meetinghouse was constructed on a two-acre parcel immediately north of the schoolhouse. The church and the school were the focal point of the community. In 1887, Jeremiah Brown and Albert Owen Shorter, both of whom had "rendered services" to Sarah Hatton Robey, purchased several five-acre parcels of land owned by the Hatton family. Jeremiah Brown served as the pastor of the new Methodist church at Chapel Hill and also taught classes at the school. (Courtesy the Thomas Collection.)

Formerly the Chapel Hill Methodist Episcopal Church, Grace Methodist is one of the oldest black Methodist churches in Southern Maryland. The first meetinghouse was built here in 1893. The Edelen, Hatton, Thorne, and Gallahan families sold the land on which this historic building stood to six blacks. In 1902, a new church was constructed to replace the original meetinghouse. The 1902 building was in use until 1975, when the present brick church was built. (Courtesy the Thomas Collection.)

In 1868, the Freedmen's Bureau established the Chapel Hill School. The school, a two-room building, also received money from the Rosenwald Fund. In 1922, a new Rosenwald school building was constructed west of and adjacent to the 50-year-old Freedmen's Bureau schoolhouse. In 1942, the Sojourner Truth School opened in Oxon Hill and the Chapel Hill students began attending the consolidated school. The Chapel Hill school closed in 1952. The old school buildings were used for a time as a community center but were eventually razed by the fire department and are no longer standing. In 1972, the Prince George's County Board of School Commissioners took over management of the school.

Seven

CHURCHES

While Lord Baltimore permitted some Jesuits to go to Maryland, in part because of the number of servants they agreed to bring in, he did not encourage their proselytizing among the non-Catholics who made up the great majority of the population. Lord Baltimore was even less inclined to favor priests after his battle with the Jesuits over land and the extra legal rights they claimed for themselves and their servants. From the time of the Act of Toleration, enacted in 1649, all Christians were in theory free to follow whatever religion they chose, though there was no tolerance for unbelievers. However, until 1692, no great attempt to build churches or to induce Protestant clergymen to come to the colony was made. When the Church of England was formally established in 1692, the bounds of the Parish of Piscataway were laid down, with the northern limit established as the "line of the Province." In January 1693, the Maryland General Assembly voted that the poll tax of 40 pounds of tobacco should be turned over to John Addison, Esquire, and William Hutchinson to pay carpenters for the building of a church on a parcel of land at Broad Creek.

St. John's Episcopal Church in Broad Creek is located on Livingston Road. In the early 18th century, the Piscataway Parish was gradually known by three different names. In 1724, it was known as King George's Parish; in 1725, the general assembly named it St. John's Parish. In 1902, the Diocese of the Washington officially named it King George's Parish, with St. John's Episcopal as the parish church. St. John's is a diverse community of believers and seekers. (Courtesy St. John's historians Jim Titus and Phyllis Cox.)

St. John's Church-Broad Creek

In 1692, the Piscataway Parish in Charles County was one of the 30 original Maryland parishes of the Church of England. The parish extended along the Potomac River from Mattawoman Creek to the upper limits of the province. Early visitors and parishioners of St. John's included George Washington; Col. John Addison, the first elected foreman of the vestry of the Piscataway Parish; John Fraser, the first rector; and Henry Addison, the son of Col. John Addison. (Courtesy St. John's historians Jim Titus and Phyllis Cox.)

St. John's Church cemetery is one of the oldest in southern Maryland. The cemetery contains several hundred markers dating from 1800 to the present day. Homemade concrete crosses, Colonial scroll-top markers, picturesque 19th-century allegorical markers, and contemporary granite markers surround the church. Many are in fair to poor condition, and some have been displaced from their original locations. Noted families throughout the Broad Creek community were buried in the cemetery. (Courtesy St. John's historians Jim Titus and Phyllis Cox.)

IGNATIUS
XON HILL, MD.

MULCAHEY—

St. Ignatius of Loyola is located in Fort Washington. In 1849, the cornerstone of the church was laid. The church was dedicated on May 2, 1850, by the Most Reverend Samuel Eccleston, Archbishop of Baltimore. The site for the church was on the old road that went from Marlboro to the ferry at Fort Foote. Since the route at that time went to Alexandria by boat, the road was called the Alexandria Ferry Road. The land was given to two Episcopalian gentlemen, Dr. Folsom and Maj. William G. Edelen. The two main people who solicited funds for the building were ladies—Mrs. Christiana S. E. Edelen and Mrs. Mary Surratt, a convert—who while soliciting rode through the countryside on horseback. Prior to 1850, the only masses celebrated in the area were in the home of Mrs. James Edelen, who at appointed times had her carriage meet Rev. Joseph Finotti at the ferry on Saturdays, kept him overnight, and had the neighbors in on Sunday for mass.

Bishop John Carroll was born in Marlborough, Maryland. He became the first Roman Catholic bishop in the United States after being elected by his fellow clergy. In November 1789, he was named bishop of Baltimore by Pope Pius VI. Carroll's new position enabled him to establish many fine schools in the nation, including Georgetown University, St. Mary's College for Boys (which became Loyola University), and Mount St. Mary's College in Emmitsburg.

Dr. Peter Heiskell married Hester Hill, a sister of Mrs. Finotti. Mrs. Finotti was the wife of Fr. Joseph Finotti's brother, Augustavo Adolfo Finotti. The Heiskells purchased Kildare, the property adjoining St. Ignatius of Loyola Church, the year after the church was built in 1850. This property formerly belonged to Dr. Folsom, who gave the land for the church. Dr. Heiskell donated the land for the hall adjoining the church. (Courtesy St. Ignatius of Loyola Roman Catholic Church Historical Publication.)

Fr. Joseph Finotti was born in Ferrara, Italy. Convinced of his calling, he went to Rome to join the Society of Jesus when he was 16. His brother was a papal count and consul of the Pope at Boston. At the founding of St. Ignatius of Loyola Church in Oxon Hill, Father Finotti was associated with St. Mary's Church in Alexandria, Virginia, and he served as pastor of Oxon Hill from 1849 until 1852. (Courtesy St. Ignatius of Loyola Roman Catholic Church Historical Publication.)

The historical church of St. Ignatius of Loyola still stands. The present pastor is Fr. Robert A. Finamore, a priest of the Archdiocese of Washington. It is still the "prettiest little Church in Southern Maryland," as stated by Cardinal Gibbons at the dedication of the new church in 1891. The church has a racially and ethnically diverse congregation who continue to offer support to the parish and school. (Courtesy St. Ignatius of Loyola Roman Catholic Church Historical Publication.)

St. Ignatius contains 20 windows donated by Dr. P. H. Heiskell, T. B. Dyer, P. H. Hill, Clement and Margaret E. Brooke, Frances and Ella May Ridgeway, Esther and Elsie Heiskell, John H. and Margaret A. Brooks, the children of Clement H. and Anne Brooke, William Strecker, the children of Julia A. Kerby, Sgt. Charles Kerby, Rachel E. Owens, the parents of Daniel J. Curtin, Fr. Thomas Hughes, Fr. Stephen J. Clark of St. Michael's Frostburg, Fr. Joseph A. Cunnane of St. Mary's Church, and Fr. D. C. de Wulf of Govanston, Maryland. (Courtesy St. Ignatius of Loyola Roman Catholic Church Historical Publication.)

The church is Romanesque, and the tower rises to a height of 80 feet. Seating capacity on the ground floor is 350, and the gallery that runs across the north end holds 50 more. The bell in the tower was cast by Henry McShane of Baltimore, is tuned to C, weighs 730 pounds, and is the joint donation of Nicholas Brooke, George H. Gray, Michel Quinn, and Fr. Thomas Hughes. (Courtesy St. Ignatius of Loyola Roman Catholic Church Historical Publication.)

This 1971 photograph represents the original eighth-grade graduating class from St. Ignatius of Loyola Catholic School, which opened in 1963. The school was a dream that became a reality for the archdiocese. The historical St. Ignatius of Loyola Roman Catholic Church still remains the place of worship in the parish. (Courtesy St. Ignatius of Loyola Roman Catholic Church Historical Publication.)

Among the distinguished Jesuits linked with the church were Fathers Finotti, Bixio, Vigilanti, Kroes, and de Necker. St. Ignatius came under the jurisdiction of the Carmelites. The church later became a mission attached to St. Dominic's Church in Washington, D.C. The Josephites also served St. Ignatius. (Courtesy St. Ignatius of Loyola Roman Catholic Church Historical Publication.)

In September 1890, Father Hughes announced plans for a new structure. On October 21, 1891, Cardinal Gibbons dedicated the new Church of St. Ignatius. St. Ignatius has been identified with St. Mary's Alexandria, St. Mary's Marlboro, St. Mary's Piscataway, St. Dominic's Washington, Holy Rosary Rosaryville, St. Theresa's Anacostia, and the Assumption Congress Heights. The church was served by Jesuits (1848–1856), Dominicans (1856–1869), Carmelites (1869–1975), Josephites (1975–1979), and Diocesans (1879–present). (Courtesy St. Ignatius Roman Catholic Church Historical Publication.)

In 1856, 13 African Americans left Mt. Zion Methodist Episcopal Church in Georgetown because of discrimination and segregation. As written by a founding member, the members wanted to "establish a church by colored folks with colored pastors . . . where [the members] would worship in dignity, spirit and truth." For a while, the church worshipped in private homes, calling themselves Beckett's Mission. Shortly thereafter, the members erected a church in Northwest Washington, D.C., and named it Ebenezer. Ebenezer means "stone of help," as referenced in 1 Samuel 7:12. Thus began a journey of faith. Over a century, the members worshipped and praised God in historic Georgetown under the leadership of distinguished pastors. By 1983, black families started leaving Georgetown for economic and political reasons. (Courtesy Ebenezer Web site [www.ebenezerame.org/history.htm] and the Woods Collection.)

With the vision, leadership, and support of the African Methodist Episcopal (AME) Church officials, 17 families moved from Georgetown to Allentown Road in Fort Washington, Maryland. Under the leadership of Rev. Dr. Grainger Browning and Rev. Dr. Jo Ann Browning, the Ebenezer family outgrew its 500-seat sanctuary and had to begin holding worship services at Friendly High School near the old church. In 1986, Ebenezer held services at the Friendly High School auditorium. In 1994, having outgrown the 1,500-seat auditorium at Friendly Ebenezer, Ebenezer carried their faith pilgrimage to Ebenezer the Beautiful, a 2,600-seat sanctuary on 33 acres of land. The "Miracle on Allentown Road" now nurtures more than 12,000 members and 100 ministries with meetings, Bible stories, and activities every day of the week. Ever mindful of the multitude of spiritual and human needs not just within the church family, but also throughout the community, Ebenezer's future plans include a school, family life center, and senior citizens complex. (Courtesy Ebenezer Web site [www.ebenezerame.org/history.htm] and the Woods Collection.)

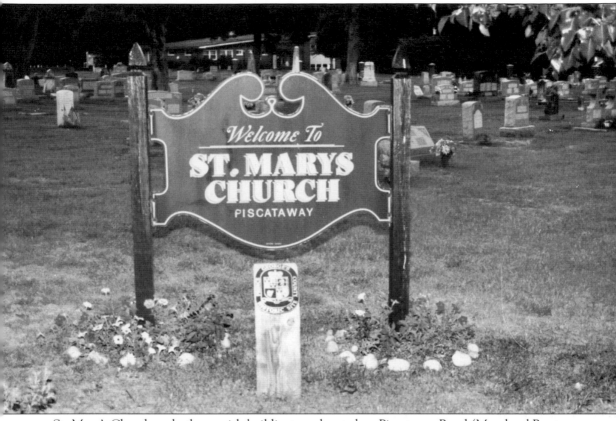

St. Mary's Church and other parish buildings are located on Piscataway Road (Maryland Route 223), at the intersection of Floral Park Road. An old chapel, a new church, a graveyard, and a school building reside on the land where Fr. Andrew White, S.J., baptized the emperor of the Piscataway Indians, Chitomachen, along with his wife, his child, and members of his tribe. (Courtesy the Thomas Collection.)

St. Mary's Catholic Church is located in the Piscataway area. Growth of Catholicism in Colonial America was slow because of repressive policies toward the faith. Wealthy Catholic families built chapels on their plantations. In 1891, St. Mary's became a mission of St. John the Evangelist in Clinton, due to St. John's prominence in the region. In 1900, the old church was condemned as unsafe, and a new church was built in 1904. (Courtesy the Thomas Collection.)

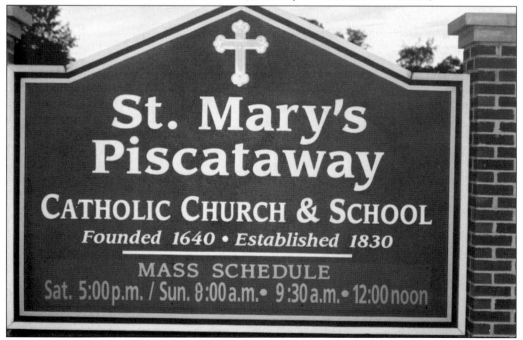

In 1838, Piscataway's first Catholic church, which took seven years to build, became operational. St. Mary's Catholic Church was located in the center of town, a few hundred feet from the Piscataway Creek and its wharf. The official register of St. Mary's began in 1874, indicating that the church held regular religious services. Early priests described the roads to Piscataway as "abominable and a disgrace."

The official recorded history of St. Mary's of Piscataway dates back to July 5, 1640. In 1900, the old church was condemned as unsafe, and a house on one-and-a-half acres was purchased in which to hold services until the new church was built in 1904. The cornerstone of the old church was placed over the door of the new church. (Courtesy the Thomas Collection.)

In 1987, St. Mary's was restored by Kerns Group. The restoration included a school addition and the conversion of existing classroom space into a library and a science room. The new church is organized on an axis featuring symbols of death and rebirth (cemetery and baptistery), fire (fireplace), water (baptistery and font), and air (natural light). A beautiful "new church" was dedicated in 1988 by James Cardinal Hickey, while the "little church" was preserved and restored. (Courtesy the Thomas Collection.)

A stroll through the graveyard recalls the names familiar to many in the southern part of the county: Barry, Boswell, Bryan, Digges, Dyer, Edelen, Gallahan, Gardiner, Gwynn, Hurtt, Jenkins, Murphy, Mudd, Parker, Queen, Underwood, and Waring. (Courtesy the Thomas Collection.)

Christ Church, built in 1747, was one of the earliest Episcopal churches in southern Maryland. Due to a fire in 1856, the church went through major renovations and repairs. The new building was rebuilt around the remaining brick walls.

In 1695, the residents of the Accokeek area established a chapel of ease for worship services without the peril of long-distance travel to St. John's in Broad Creek. Christ Church's boundaries run from Piscataway Creek on the north to Mattawoman Creek on the south. Christ Church was one of the six pre-Revolutionary churches built by the Church of England. The rector of Broad Creek held services three times a month. (Sketch courtesy Sarah Parker.)

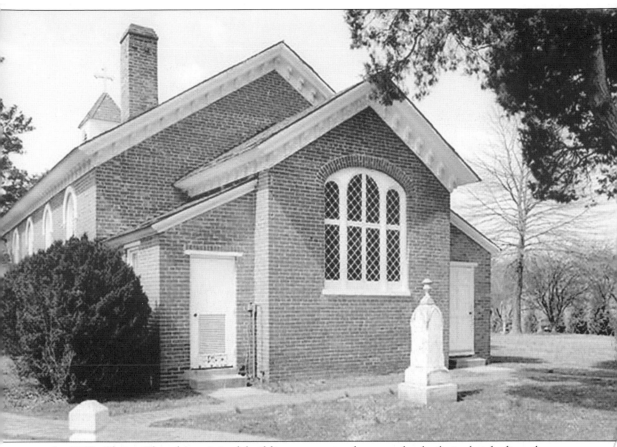

In 1745, Christ Church's original building was torn down and rebuilt in brick directly on the ground, with no footings or foundation. The design of the early church was dictated by the theology of the times, which did not permit music during Holy Services, nor did it allow decorative colored or stained-glass church windows. (Courtesy Christ Church Web site [http://christchurchaccokeek.edow.org/].)

Christ Church–Accokeek's parish remained on private land until December 14, 1843, at which time William Henry Lyles and his wife, Elizabeth C. Lyles, deeded the southern section of their farm, Cherry Mount, to the church, which paid $75 for the property. In 1823, the congregation received recognition as a separate parish. In 1869, a separate congregation named St. John's Parish was formed from it. The growth of Christ Church has paralleled the population increase of the Accokeek area. A rectory was built on the property in 1932. A multipurpose room was added in 1961. In 1968, restoration returned the building to the 1857 style while using the hexagonal brick floor of 1745. (Courtesy HABS, Library of Congress, Prints and Photographs Division.)

Eight

PEOPLE, PLACES, AND NEIGHBORHOODS

The Fort Washington area represents a diversity of people, places, and neighborhoods encompassing many cultural and ethnic groups who live in a harmonious environment. Progress has had many advantages as well as disadvantages. Neighborhoods such as Historic Broad Creek and Chapel Hill suffered greatly with overcrowding of schools and recreational facilities. Chapel Hill, a post–Civil War African American community, was divided by the development of Indian Head Highway (Maryland Route 210). With the invention of the automobile, people began to move away from farms, the region's major industry, and started commuting to work in Washington, D.C., and other local governments. As developers purchased large farms and established several affluent subdivisions, the fabric of the Fort Washington community began to change. With the formation of Tantallon Estates as a model, other subdivisions such as Battersea and Riverview were established to create an air of dignity and status. Residents of the region today include teachers, postal workers, nurses, doctors, dentists, and government workers at all levels. Professionals such as Dr. Henry DiLorenzo, politicians such as Sen. Gloria Lawlah and Councilman Tony Knotts, and entrepreneurs Ollie P. Anderson Jr., president of South County Economic Development Association, Inc. (SCEDA), and Carolyn Corpening Collins Rowe, president of the Afro-American Historical and Genealogical Society (AAHGS), both work and live in the Fort Washington area. William E. Miller, a longtime county resident and well-known harness driver, turned part of his breeding farm, W. E. Miller Stables, into Rosecroft Raceway. In 1968, the Maryland–National Capital Parks and Planning Commission opened its first community center to provide leisure services to the Prince George's County community. Some of the centers are freestanding buildings, and others are housed in schools. Each center offers classes, programs, drop-in activities, and special events for people of all ages.

In 1654, Oliver Cromwell deeded the land that includes Fort Washington to his physician, Dr. Luke Barber. During the next three centuries, the area remained a quiet backwater community of the nation's capital. In the early 1960s, the Isle of Thye Land Company began to develop building and estate-style sites. Tantallon, in its earlier days, had virtually all white residents. Today the community is more diverse, and the population has increased from 7,645 to 23,845. Tantallon is still one of the wealthiest areas of Prince George's County. (Courtesy the Thomas Collection.)

Tantallon North is a comfortable, quiet, and well-maintained residential neighborhood situated in a bedroom community accessible from Fort Washington, Swan Creek, and River View Roads. There are over 500 single-family brick homes in this community. This community consists of Prince George's County's most affluent and talented African Americans—doctors, educators, entrepreneurs, historians, law enforcement officers, lawyers, ministers, and retirees, as well as government professionals. (Courtesy the Thomas Collection.)

Tantallon Country Club is located on St. Andrews Drive in Fort Washington, Maryland. The club is surrounded by million-dollar homes, a golf course, and historic sites. The spacious banquet facilities cater to special events. The club offers a variety of facilities, including swimming, a clubhouse bar and restaurant, and a ballroom and conference facility capable of holding large crowds. (Courtesy the Thomas Collection.)

Tantallon Country Golf Course is located in the Tantallon community of Fort Washington. Avid golfers can enjoy the greenery of the Tantallon Country Golf Course. This beautifully landscaped 18-hole course is one of most popular courses in the Washington metropolitan area. The club features carts, a driving range, a pro shop, a snack bar, and a junior golf program. Fort Washington is a private golf club that offers members and guests an enjoyable golf experience. (Courtesy the Thomas Collection.)

Dr. Henry DiLorenzo, D.D.S., is an orthodontist and a longtime resident of Tantallon. He is a graduate of Georgetown University (1957–1960). Dr. DiLorenzo received his dental degree from Georgetown Dental School (1960–1964). He is married to Marion Douglass and is the proud father of four children: Daniel, M.D., Ph.D., and M.B.A.; Michael, prosecutor for the U.S. Department of Justice; Nicole, a high school guidance counselor; and Chris, a dental school student. In his spare time, Dr. DiLorenzo enjoys fishing, boating, hunting, and traveling.

Since 1974, Dr. DiLorenzo has practiced orthodontic dentistry in Charles and Prince George's Counties. He is very active in community and professional associations such as the Georgetown Orthodontic Foundation, Southern Maryland Dental Association, and the Patuxent Dental Society of Maryland. Dr. DiLorenzo has received several service awards and served as president of a Kiwanis club, a home and school association, and a sportsmen's club, and he was a committee chairman and badge counselor for the Boy Scouts of America.

Potomac Landing Community Center is located in the Potomac Landing Elementary School in the Tantallon area. This center offers indoor and outdoor amenities. Recreation programs and classes are among the activities offered in the center. The center also hosts camps, special events, workshops, drop-in programs, after-school programs, and cultural activities at different times. (Courtesy the Thomas Collection.)

Tucker Road Community Center is a freestanding facility located on Tucker Road in the Henson Creek Stream Valley Park. It is one of 40 centers providing leisure services, recreation programs, and an assortment of classes to the Prince George's County community. The center offers citizens a fitness room, gymnasium, meeting rooms, restrooms, and kitchens. Outdoor recreation facilities include a picnic area, two lighted tennis courts, play equipment, and two sand volleyball courts. (Courtesy the Thomas Collection.)

River View

In 1866, Capt. Ephraim S. Randall built River View on Hatton Point. The property featured a 250-acre park. River View was a popular resort, and excursion boats ferried day-trippers along the Potomac. William B. Emmert purchased River View at auction for $23,000 in 1909. In 1920, Col. James Gillespie, a quartermaster at Fort Washington, bought River View for use as a residence. The present owners restored the outdoor porches and walks to their original configuration. (Courtesy Sarah Parker, *Along the Potomac Shore in Prince George's County.*)

Indian Queen Recreation Center, located on Fort Foote Road, is housed in the Indian Queen Elementary School. The facility includes a gymnasium shared with the school, staff office space, a storage area, restrooms, and some use of the school's classrooms. The families in the community can use the athletic fields, basketball court, and play equipment located outside the school. Recreation programs and classes, after-school programs, special events, and drop-in activities are offered at this facility. (Courtesy the Thomas Collection.)

Silesia School-The First One

Silesia School, a historic one-story school building, was built in 1902. In the 1930s, it was enlarged and converted to dwellings. In 1885, Robert Stein, a translator, explorer, and author, purchased a 320-acre parcel of land at Livingston and Fort Washington Roads and named the area Silesia after Silesia, Prussia. Robert's brother Richard and Joseph Adler joined Robert, and the families operated a grocery and feed store eventually owned by a cousin, Joseph Tilch. Joseph's nephew, Robert, operated the business from 1911 until his death in January 1974.

In 1984, the Oxon Hill Recreation and Cultural Council, in commemoration of Maryland's 350th birthday, donated the Oxon Hill Fitness Trail as part of the Tucker Road Sports Complex. The complex is home to a 19-station physical fitness "Exer-Trail." The system is approximately one mile long within a park setting in the southern portion of Prince George's County. (Courtesy the Thomas Collection)

In 1947, William E. Miller, a celebrated driver and horse breeder, established the Rosecroft Raceway on Brinkley Road in Oxon Hill. For more than 50 years, Rosecroft Raceway led the harness racing tracks of Maryland. It is the only known raceway owned by an organization consisting of owners, trainers, and drivers of harness racehorses participating in Maryland. Miller was a 50-year career driver and winner of many county fairs and pari-mutuel races in New York, New Jersey, Delaware, and Pennsylvania. (Courtesy Jo Proctor, Rosecroft Raceway.)

On November 30, 1995, the Maryland–National Capital Parks and Planning Commission paid tribute to Rosa Lee Blumenthal by dedicating a sports complex in her honor. From 1987 to 1994, Blumenthal served as a member of the Maryland House of Delegates, representing the 26th Legislative District of Fort Washington. Delegate Blumenthal actively served on the Oxon Hill Recreation and Cultural Council and the Prince George's Federation of Park and Recreation Councils, which support parks and recreation. (Courtesy the Thomas Collection.)

William E. Miller, founder and owner of Rosecroft Raceway, drove his first race in 1907 at the old Brightwood Track near Washington, D.C. He died of a heart attack while driving Josedale Mate at the Harrington, Delaware, track at the age of 70. Mr. Miller was nominated to the Horsemen's Hall of Fame in 1976. (Courtesy Rosecroft Raceway.)

Rosecroft Raceway started out as part of the W. E. Miller Stables. The stables were part of the Rosecroft Stock Farm for breeding racehorses. Rosecroft is a member of the Prince George's County Chamber of Commerce and SCEDA. The raceway is very active in the community, hosting family festivals, fund-raisers, and flea markets, and working with churches and the fire and police departments. Other community activities include an annual Senior Citizen Day and fund-raisers for politicians. Rosecroft Raceway breeds Standardbred yearlings and trains jockeys. (Courtesy Rosecroft Raceway.)

The Maryland Governor's Cup
REDNECK BUBBA

June 4 1999
Driver: Allan Davis
Owner: Edwin C. Bartley

1:56:4

New Mark

$15,000.00
2nd: Impeccable Image
3rd: Super Tan

Rosecroft established a Governor's Day celebration. Here is Gov. Parris Glendening and some members of his staff at Rosecroft, where they enjoyed a day of fun and races. (Courtesy Rosecroft Raceway.)

Rosecroft hosts the Family FunFeast the last Saturday of June for children of all ages. Rosecroft provides free food, drinks, a moon bounce, games, and pony rides. The feast is a day-long affair that begins at noon and ends about 8:00 p.m. A fireworks display ends the day's festivities.

Rosecroft hosts an annual yearlings sale of the best Maryland Standardbred horses every October. The Standardbred horse is often described as "honest." He is robust, plain, rugged, and capable of performing any job, and he is one of the equine world's best-kept secrets. He is the fastest harness-racing breed. These yearlings, between their first and second birthday, are the descendants of the best of Maryland's horseflesh.

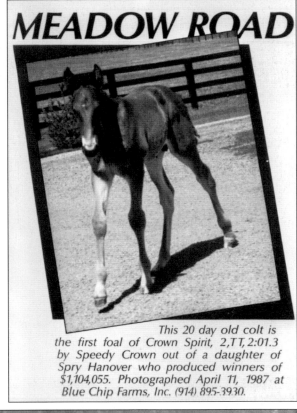

This 20 day old colt is the first foal of Crown Spirit, 2,TT, 2:01.3 by Speedy Crown out of a daughter of Spry Hanover who produced winners of $1,104,055. Photographed April 11, 1987 at Blue Chip Farms, Inc. (914) 895-3930.

Laurel Raceway celebrated its anniversary on this special day at Rosecroft. This was a joint celebration of harness racing at Laurel, which began in 1948, one year before Rosecroft opened.

Law Enforcement Day was established to benefit the Law Enforcement Memorial Fund. It is an annual affair open to all law enforcement departments within the Washington metropolitan area. The fund-raising activity benefits the families of fallen law officers.

Horse racing at Rosecroft Raceway has been an enjoyable pastime since Colonial times, when owners of plantations and farms raced their best horses against each other. In 1879, the term Standardbred was introduced to distinguish those trotting horses who met a certain time standard over a mile. Harness racing is governed by the United States Trotting Association and uses Standardbred horses exclusively as trotters.

Rosecroft Raceway is one of two harness race tracks in the great state of Maryland. In addition to hosting daily races, the track is also open Thursday, Friday, and Saturday nights. Rosecroft is also a well-known facility for training and breeding Standardbred horses. Trainers and jockeys can live on the property year-round.

The Tantallon Yacht Club, complete with a marina and private slips, is located on Swan Creek Road. It was designed for a community that enjoys water sports such as sailing, boating, and fishing. The club is a member of the Potomac River Yacht Clubs Association (PRYCA). Members of the club participate in the PRYCA annual delegates meeting, dinner dance, races, and other boating activities. (Courtesy the Thomas Collection.)

Rosecroft Raceway is one of two harness racetracks in Maryland; the other is at Ocean Downs in Berlin. Rosecroft is conveniently located off the Capital Beltway at St. Barnabas Road, a short distance from Washington, D.C. Rosecroft also hosts the Sire Stake Races. The Sire Stake Races are designed to promote Standardbred breeding and racing within the state of Maryland.

In 1969, William E. Miller (right) and friends celebrated the 20th anniversary of Rosecroft with cake and other refreshments. It was a festive occasion, and special races were held.

Rosecroft is a full-service racetrack that holds races throughout the year. In conjunction with Colonial Downs in Virginia, Rosecroft closes the track for a period of six weeks from September to October each year. Rosecroft serves dinner and drinks during the races. Customers can even watch other races across the country through off-track betting and Simulcast.

Masonry stone, surrounded by beautiful manicured landscaping, marks the entrance to the upscale dwellings of Potomac Knolls. The community, bordered by Maryland Route 210 and Old Fort Road, includes several hundred multi-story homes occupied by upper-middle class families. The Potomac Knolls community is close to several shopping centers. One of its most notable residents is the president of SCEDA, Ollie P. Anderson Jr. (Courtesy the Thomas Collection.)

WARW - 94.7 FM PACE
BEACH SCOOTER
1:54

October 9 1999
Driver: John Wagner
Owner: Michael S. Aspiotis

$6,500.00
2nd: Cry Uncle
3rd: Distant Game

The last Saturday in June is Fun Day at Rosecroft. The annual community fest includes fun and games, pony rides, food, and fireworks. Rosecroft works with community leaders and politicians in planning the affair. Rosecroft is very involved with community activities and is available for private parties and weddings.

The Potomac Knolls Community Center is a lovely two-story building surrounded by a beautiful landscape of flowers and trees. The center provides accessible space for community activities and programs raising awareness through public education, art, and political forums; regular meetings of the Potomac Knolls Civic Association; and a place for neighbors to hold private celebrations, weddings, and other programs. Its location and design promote the full inclusion of all people of diverse backgrounds. (Courtesy the Thomas Collection.)

Fort Washington Marina is nestled on the Potomac River and borders Fort Washington National Park. In the summer, locals jet ski on the river, moor boats on private docks, and enjoy views of Independence Day fireworks. The area marina serves as a vacation home, weekend getaway, or a homeport for many residents and families in the surrounding area. Boat access to Piscataway Creek and the Potomac River are available at Fort Washington Marina for a fee. The marina also has a restroom and some vending machines. (Courtesy the Thomas Collection.)

Capitol Sailboat Club is an official American Sailing Association sailing school. The school has several locations, one of which is the Fort Washington Marina. For those new to the sport, the school offers an introductory course that familiarizes new sailors with boat, rigging, and sailing concepts. Upon successful completion, trainees have a basic working knowledge of keelboats and the ability to take the helm of a sailboat about 20 feet in length in light to moderate winds. (Courtesy the Thomas Collection.)

Proud Mary Restaurant and Tiki Bar is located on the Potomac River at the Fort Washington Marina. Proud Mary offers its guests delectable meals and gracious service at lunch or dinner. Whether customers arrive by land or sea, lunch or dinner satisfies appetites in the dining room or on the waterfront deck. In the evening, customers enjoy the breathtaking view of the Potomac River while listening to fantastic entertainment. (Courtesy the Thomas Collection.)

Colonial Piscataway Tavern, built in the mid-18th century, was a two-and-a-half-story, gable-roofed frame house attached to an older, one-and-a-half-story section. The Piscataway Tavern was owned and operated by Mrs. Catherine Playfay throughout the 18th century. The tavern was located on a road near Broad Creek and served as a stagecoach stop for the ferry to Alexandria, Virginia.

The Piscataway Tavern provided food, shelter, and care for travel-weary passengers and horses. The tavern consisted of a taproom, parlor, and dining room with sleeping accommodations for guests. George Washington was said to have been a frequent customer on his way to Washington, D.C. This picture was taken in 1936 by the Historic American Buildings Survey. The Piscataway Tavern was a center for recreation where farmers heard news of the outside world. The Piscataway tavern also hosted public meetings when needed.

Henson Creek Trail, located in the southern portion of Prince George's County, is a part of the Maryland–National Capital Parks and Planning Commission. Henson Creek Trail extends just over six miles from Temple Hill Road southward to Oxon Hill Road, crossing Indian Head Highway before reaching its southern terminus. The trail travels through Henson Creek Neighborhood Park, crossing several major roads, including Brinkley Road, through the Henson Creek Stream Valley Park, passing Rosecroft Raceway and the Tucker Road Community Park. (Courtesy the Thomas Collection.)

Piscataway House

Piscataway House, also known as Collins House, was originally built in the town of Piscataway and sat next to Hardy's Tavern on the south side, near St. John's Episcopal Church. Piscataway House is now a private residence. James Wilfong described Piscataway House as "a representative of Southern Maryland's eighteenth century building in its purest primitive form because of the double chimneys with windowless panes on both sides of the house, and due to its long sloping roof line with its finely proportioned dormers." In January 1932, Charles Collins acquired the property from the Sellners, and he moved Piscataway House to its present location on Livingston Road when a road-widening project threatened the house. In 1956, the property was purchased by Gen. George Brown, Air Force chief of staff. Mr. and Mrs. Carroll Savage also owned the property and made many additions. According to Mr. Savage, Piscataway House was known as the old haunted Marshall House, and some visitors have heard odd noises. There is a Georgetown-style courtyard leading to the main house. The connecting wing to the left of the house has been added, as well as a swimming pool at the back of the house. The historical front of the house faces the river. Piscataway House is an important link in the historic chain to the past along Livingston Road in the Fort Washington area.

Nine

FORT FOOTE

In May 1863, Fort Foote was constructed with the latest naval defense technology, designed to be one of 68 temporary field fortifications. Fort Foote constituted one of the Civil War defenses of Washington built to resist the attack of ground forces. The fort was a seacoast fortification and built to resist moisture and naval shells. Fort Foote is located on Rozier's Bluff approximately eight miles below Washington. A large swamp plagued the post with malaria during the summer, and the lack of pure water made typhoid a constant threat. Less than 200 officers and men were garrisoned at the fort during the Civil War. The fort's primary focus was to guard the river route to Alexandria, Washington, and Georgetown. The fort and surrounding facilities were not completed until 1865. After the death of Rear Adm. Andrew Hull Foote, Secretary of State William H. Seward dedicated and named the fort for the fallen naval hero. Along with Fort Washington, it was part of the capital's defenses against Confederate sympathizers in Northern Virginia and southern Maryland. Foot Foote was abandoned in 1878. From 1902 through 1917, the post was used as a practice area for students from the engineer school. The fort was briefly reactivated during World War I. During World War II, Fort Washington used the post for training officer candidates. Fort Foote was transferred to the Department of the Interior under the Capper-Crampton Act and is now a part of the National Park Service. It is considered to be one of the most well preserved of all the defenses built around Washington in the Civil War. The fort's remnants, now a local park, contain Rodman guns and other remnants.

A directional sign leads visitors to the historic Fort Foote, whose entrance is located on Old Fort Road off Indian Head Highway. Eight miles downriver from the capital, Fort Foote was considered "a powerful enclosed work" by its chief engineer "and the most elaborate . . . of all the defenses of Washington." The long oval earthwork was constructed on Rozier's Bluff from 1863 to 1865 to strengthen the ring of fortifications that encircled Washington, D.C., during the Civil War. (Courtesy the Thomas Collection.)

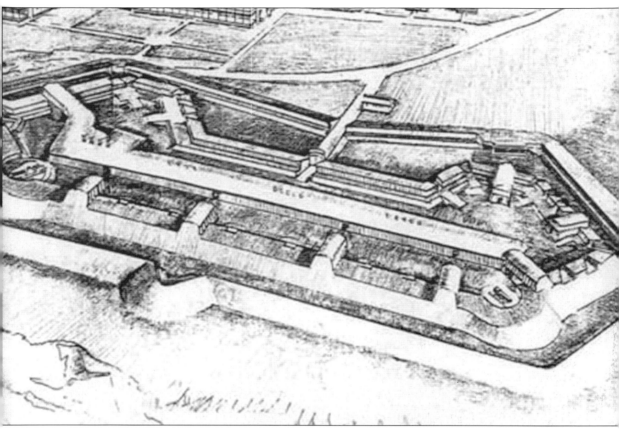

Fort Foote was one of 68 temporary earth and log structures designed to resist the attack of ground forces such as infantry, cavalry, and artillery. The front of the fort was over 500 feet long, and the earth walls were 20 feet thick. A central traverse ran the length of the fort and contained bombproof magazines and storage areas. Fort Foote was designed to protect the river entrance to the ports of Alexandria, Georgetown, and Washington, and to replace the aging Fort Washington as the primary river defense. Fort Foote was a seacoast fortification, which engineers maintained to insure that the fort could resist moisture and naval shells.

Fort Foote was named for Rear Adm. Andrew Hull Foote (1806–1863), who distinguished himself in actions against Confederate forts on the Mississippi River and died of his wounds on June 26, 1863.

This photograph shows a 15-inch Rodman gun. With a deafening roar, the Rodman cannon could hurl 440-pound shells three miles. Companies of the 9th New York Heavy Artillery worked to build and arm the fort. The last in the ring of forts and batteries to be abandoned when peacetime returned, Fort Foote continued in active status until 1878. It was briefly reactivated as a training site during World War I.

The post was used as a practice area for students from the engineer school from 1902 through 1917. Most of the guns were removed, but one of Fort Foote's Parrott rifles was sent to the Evergreen Cemetery in Leechburg, Pennsylvania. It now stands guard over the remains of 20 Civil War soldiers buried there. (Courtesy National Park Service.)

The Fort Washington National Park is a 341-acre park open to the public for tours, reenactments, picnics, and other recreational activities. This breathtaking landscape view of a side of the fort shows a vast acreage of trees and other vegetation off the Potomac River. The park includes bike and hiking paths visible from this view leading right down to the shoreline. (Courtesy the Thomas Collection.)

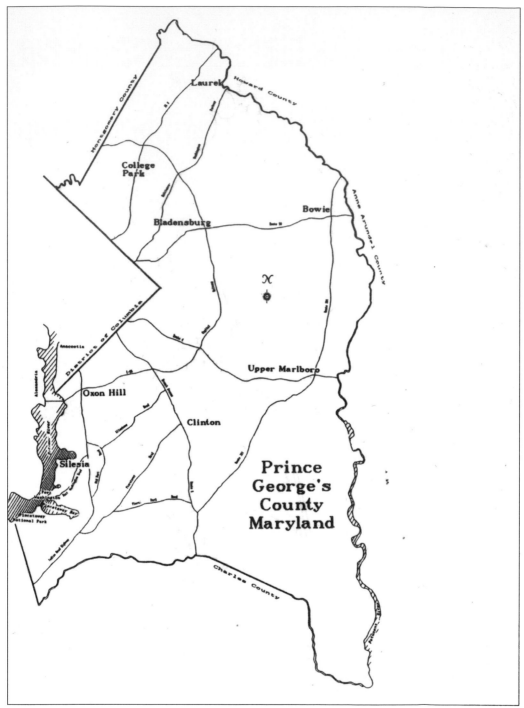

A map of Prince George's County illustrates the southern end of the county along the Potomac River. The Piscataway Creek leads into the Potomac River along the Maryland and Virginia shorelines. In 1696, the Maryland General Assembly created Prince George's County, named for Prince George of England, from St. Mary's and Charles Counties. Fort Washington is one of the fastest growing communities in the county.